# CONTENTS

# CHAPTER 1

# MATTER ALL AROUND US

Matter is all around us. Trees, water, air, the Moon ...

AWOO!

... and werewolves are all made of matter. Matter is anything that takes up space and has mass.

mass the amount of matter in an object

4

MASS: 100Kg
WEIGHT: 100Kg

Wherever a werewolf goes, his total mass does not change. Weight measures the pull of gravity on an object. Earth's gravity is stronger than the Moon's. The werewolf weighs more on Earth than on the Moon. However, his mass remains the same.

MASS: 100Kg
WEIGHT: 16.5Kg

gravity force that pulls objects together

CHOCOL RABBITS

RECIPE

## VOLUME

The amount of space an object takes up is measured as its volume. Liquid volumes are usually measured in units such as litres. Solid volumes are usually measured in units such as cubic centimetres ($cm^3$).

One way to study matter is to observe its properties. Some properties can be measured, such as height and weight.

Other properties describe how matter looks or feels. Tongue depressors are flat and smooth.

SAY AAHH!

A doctor's reflex hammer is hard.

Toc

A doctor's ear scope can be cold.

BRR!

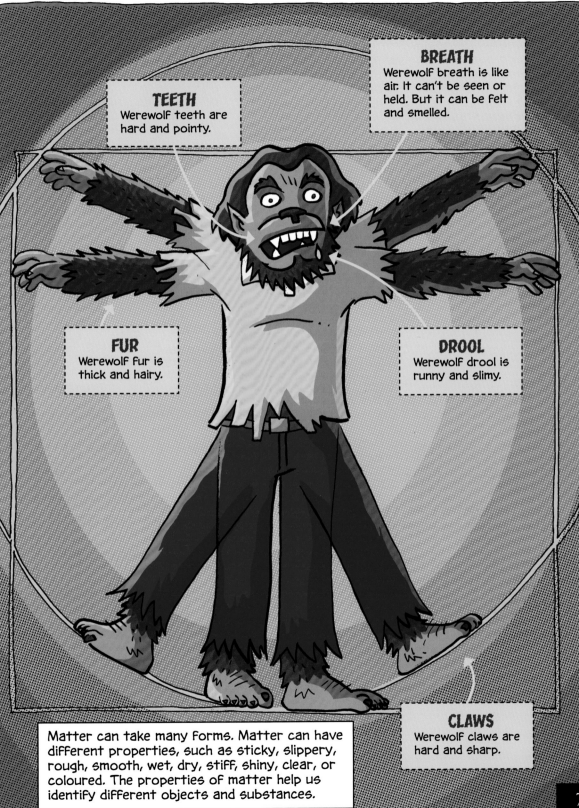

**BREATH**
Werewolf breath is like air. It can't be seen or held. But it can be felt and smelled.

**TEETH**
Werewolf teeth are hard and pointy.

**FUR**
Werewolf fur is thick and hairy.

**DROOL**
Werewolf drool is runny and slimy.

**CLAWS**
Werewolf claws are hard and sharp.

Matter can take many forms. Matter can have different properties, such as sticky, slippery, rough, smooth, wet, dry, stiff, shiny, clear, or coloured. The properties of matter help us identify different objects and substances.

# CHAPTER 2

# STATES OF MATTER

Another way to study matter is to observe its state. Most of the matter on Earth exists in one of three states: solid, liquid, or gas. All three states of matter can be found in a werewolf.

MY, WHAT BIG TEETH YOU HAVE!

state the form of a substance

A tooth is solid. It does not easily change shape, and its volume doesn't change.

Drool is a liquid. It takes the shape of the container that holds it. Its volume doesn't change unless the werewolf drools more.

IF YOU MUST DROOL, PLEASE USE A CUP.

Breath is a gas. It only holds its shape within a container. The volume of a gas can change, even inside a container.

Liquids and gases are called fluids. A fluid is a substance that flows. Drool flows out of a cup when you pour it. Breath can flow like a breeze from a blown-up rubber glove.

# PLASMA

A fourth state of matter is called plasma. Stars like the Sun are made of plasma. It is the most common state of matter in the universe. Plasma is a gas that has been highly energised. When a fluorescent light bulb is lit, the gas inside becomes plasma.

Matter doesn't stay in one state all the time. Matter changes from one state to another depending on temperature and pressure.

The temperature at which a liquid freezes is called its freezing point. At its freezing point, liquid water turns into solid ice.

IS THAT A **WEREWOLF?**

When it warms up, the ice on a frozen werewolf turns back into liquid water. The temperature at which a solid melts is called its melting point. The melting point of a substance is the same as its freezing point.

TH-TH-TH-**THANKS.**

Cold water on a wet werewolf evaporates into the air.

Water evaporates even faster when it reaches its boiling point. When water boils, water vapour escapes into the air as steam.

evaporate change from a liquid to a gas

When water vapour hits a cold surface, such as the roof of a cave, it cools and condenses. A werewolf sitting under the roof is likely to get wet.

SORRY, WE DON'T HAVE AN UMBRELLA. HAVE SOME HOT TEA INSTEAD.

condense change from a gas to a liquid

11

# CHAPTER 3

# MOLECULES AND ATOMS

All matter is made up of tiny particles called molecules. Molecules are too small to see, even under a microscope. One drop of water contains billions of molecules.

**LOOKS LIKE IT MUST BE RAINING OUTSIDE!**

molecule the smallest particle of a substance

ATOM

Molecules are made up of atoms. Atoms are the smallest building blocks of matter.

The chemical name for water is $H_2O$. Water gets its name from the atoms in a water molecule. Each water molecule has two hydrogen atoms and one oxygen atom. Water, ice, and steam are all made up of the same water molecules.

HMM, WEREWOLF DROOL IS A LOT LIKE WATER.

Different substances have different densities. For example, helium is less dense than oxygen.

density amount of mass a substance has based on its volume

A helium balloon will float because it is less dense than the air around it. But an oxygen balloon will sink because it is more dense than the air.

The molecules for a substance are the same in its solid, liquid, and gas forms. But the molecules behave differently in each state.

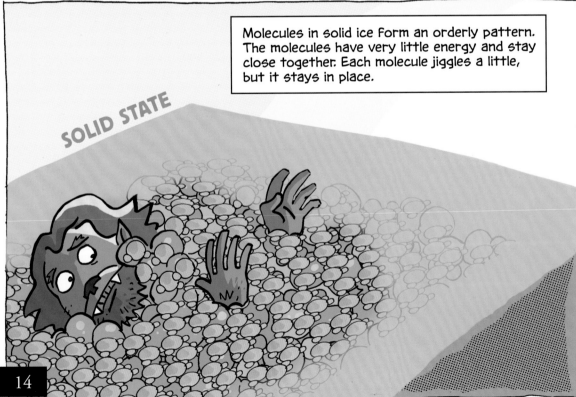

Molecules in solid ice form an orderly pattern. The molecules have very little energy and stay close together. Each molecule jiggles a little, but it stays in place.

SOLID STATE

Molecules in liquid water stay close together, but they do not form a pattern. The liquid molecules have more energy. Each molecule jiggles and moves, sliding past the other liquid molecules.

LIQUID STATE

Molecules in steam spread out rapidly. The gas molecules have a lot of energy. The molecules jiggle and zoom around. They even bounce off one another.

GAS STATE

Temperature also affects the way molecules move. At room temperature, the air molecules inside a basketball move around a lot. The ball is inflated and bounces well.

In cold temperatures, the air molecules behave differently. They stay closer together and move more slowly. The volume of the air is less than at room temperature. The ball deflates and does not bounce well.

TOO C-C-COLD FOR B-B-B-BASKETBALL.

SPLAT

SPLAT

If the ball gets hot, the air molecules inside move much faster. The volume of the air increases. If the volume increases more than the ball can hold, the ball bursts.

POW

Solids expand when they get hot, too. The expansion is often so small we don't see it. A hot rock usually looks the same as a cold rock. But if you touch it, you're in for a surprise.

AWOOO!!

## MELTING ROCKS

As a solid nears its melting point, the molecules jiggle faster and faster until they break free. When this happens, the solid melts into a liquid. Even rocks will melt if they reach their melting point. Lava from a volcano is really melted rock.

TIME TO LEAVE!

# CHAPTER 4

# MIXTURES

Matter can be combined to make a mixture. In a mixture, each substance keeps its unique physical properties. To make rabbit stew, a werewolf might make a mixture of potatoes, carrots, rabbits, and water.

You can use the physical properties of each piece to separate it from the mixture. A strainer can separate the liquids from the solids. Orange carrots look different from furry rabbits and white potatoes.

YOU CAN'T PUT A WHOLE RABBIT IN THERE!

REALLY?

Liquids and gases can form mixtures, too. A werewolf can make fruit punch by mixing different fruit juices together.

Fizzy drinks are a mixture of liquid water and carbon dioxide gas. The carbon dioxide gives the drink its fizz.

BURP

Rabbit stew combines liquids with solids. Rabbit meat and vegetables mix with juices and water to make a tasty meal.

IT SMELLS **DELICIOUS!**

A solution is a mixture in which a soluble substance is dissolved. It may look like the dissolved substance has disappeared, but it is still there.

One solution can be made by dissolving sugar in water. The sugar can't be seen, but it can be tasted.

soluble can be dissolved

Some mixtures, such as tea, are made with insoluble items. Items that are less dense float on top. Denser items sink to the bottom.

TRY SOME OF MY SPECIAL TEA BLEND.

insoluble cannot be dissolved

Small, insoluble items mixed in water make a suspension. Over time, the insoluble items settle out of the water and sink to the bottom. Crushed tea leaves form a suspension in hot water.

I PREFER A SIMPLER TEA.

suspension substance in which many particles are suspended

Insoluble items can be removed from a suspension using a strainer. The water passes through the strainer, but the insoluble tea leaves do not.

THIS IS TEA-RIFFIC!

Soluble substances dissolve completely. Both salt and sugar dissolve easily in water. But don't trust a werewolf to tell the difference.

Small sugar crystals dissolve quickly in hot water. They dissolve slowly in cold water.

But they will dissolve faster if the water is stirred quickly.

When no more sugar can be dissolved in the tea, it has reached its saturation point.

THERE'S JUST NOTHING LIKE A NICE, SWEET CUPPA.

saturation point level at which no more of a substance can by absorbed by another substance

If the tea is left alone and uncovered, the water evaporates and leaves the sugar behind. It makes a tasty treat for a werewolf.

# CHAPTER 5

# REVERSIBLE AND IRREVERSIBLE CHANGES

**HEY, GREAT COSTUME!**

Reversible changes are physical changes in matter that can be undone. Changes in state are reversible. Werewolves can make a reversible change by wearing fancy dress to a party.

Water changes into ice when it freezes. This change is reversed when the ice melts back into water.

Some changes cannot be undone. Before it is baked, cake batter is a thick, sticky liquid.

Irreversible changes are chemical changes that happen on a molecular level.

When it is baked, the cake batter can't be turned back into its ingredients. They become a different substance.

Cooking the ingredients changes the cake batter's chemical make-up. The batter's properties also change. It becomes a solid and can be eaten as a tasty treat.

Many substances can undergo both reversible and irreversible changes. Only the reversible changes can be undone.

**STAY STILL!**

Clay can be moulded into different shapes. The moist clay is soft and undergoes reversible changes. A werewolf can change the clay's shape as often as he wants.

When the clay is baked, it looks the same as before. But the molecules in the clay are changed.

The clay has become hard, and its shape can no longer be changed.

NO! I'M BETTER LOOKING THAN THAT!

Matter makes up our bodies and is found all around us. It can take many forms. Solid matter is found in an ice cube. Liquid matter makes up water. The air we breathe is made of gaseous matter.

Matter is always changing its state. Solid ice cubes melt to make liquid water. Liquid water evaporates into a gas when heated. And water vapour turns into liquid water when it is cooled.

Some changes to matter are irreversible. If a piece of paper is burned, it turns into smoke, ash, and gases. It can't be turned back into paper.

But some changes to matter are reversible. Werewolves change back into human form when the sun comes up.

However, although he looks human, he is still a werewolf. When the Moon is full, he will once again be a furry beast.

THANK GOODNESS! THAT FUR ITCHES!

# GLOSSARY

**condense** change from a gas into a liquid

**density** amount of mass an object or substance has based on a unit of volume

**evaporate** change from a liquid into a gas

**fluid** liquid or gas substance that flows

**gravity** force that pulls objects with mass together

**insoluble** cannot be dissolved in another substance

**mass** amount of material in an object

**matter** anything that has weight and takes up space

**molecule** smallest particle of a substance that can exist and still keep the characteristics of the substance

**plasma** a highly charged state of matter

**saturation point** level at which a substance cannot absorb more of another substance

**soluble** can be dissolved in another substance

**solution** mixture made of a substance that has been dissolved in another substance

**state** form a substance takes, such as solid, liquid, or gas

**suspension** substance in which many particles are suspended. Particles in a suspension can be separated.

**volume** amount of space taken up by an object or substance

# FIND OUT MORE

## BOOKS

*Changing States: Solids, Liquids, and Gases* (Do It Yourself), Will Hurd (Heinemann Library, 2010)

*Experiments with Solids, Liquids, and Gases* (True Books) Christine Taylor-Butler (Scholastic, 2011)

*Solids, Liquids, and Gases* (Superscience) Jillian Powell (Franklin Watts, 2010)

*State of Confusion: Solids, Liquids, and Gases*, Buffy Silverman (Raintree, 2007)

*The Solid Truth about States of Matter with Max Axiom, Super Scientist* (Graphic Science), Agnieszka Biskup (Raintree, 2011)

## WEBSITES

www.bbc.co.uk/schools/scienceclips/ages/10_11/rev_irrev_changes.shtml
Try a fun quiz to see how much you know about reversible and irreversible changes.

www.bbc.co.uk/schools/ks2bitesize/science/materials
Play games, find out more, and do quizzes about materials on the pages of this website.

# INDEX